ACTS OF DEVOTION

ACTS OF DEVOTION

Second Edition

GATHERED
OR PREPARED
BY
GEORGE APPLETON

LONDON
S·P·C·K
1963

First edition published in 1928
Second edition, revised, 1963
S·P·C·K
Holy Trinity Church
Marylebone Road
London N.W.1

Printed in Great Britain by
The Talbot Press (S.P.C.K.)
Saffron Walden, Essex

Contents

Acknowledgements

Thanks are due to the following for permission to include copyright material:

The B.B.C.—*New Every Morning.*

Burns and Oates, Ltd, and P. J. Kenedy and Sons—*The Life that is Light,* by Archbishop Goodier.

The Central Board of Finance of the Church of England—*The Prayer Book as proposed in 1928.*

The Church of Scotland.

The Right Reverend D. H. Crick.

The Edinburgh House Press.

The Epworth Press.

Hodder & Stoughton Ltd.—The Moffatt Bible.

The Industrial Christian Fellowship.

The Executors of the Very Reverend E. Milner-White—*My God my Glory* and *A Procession of Passion Prayers.*

The Mothers' Union.

A. R. Mowbray & Co. Ltd.—*The Prayer Manual,* by F. B. Macnutt.

The Oxford University Press—*A Diary of Private Prayer,* by John Baillie, and *Daily Prayer,* ed. E. Milner-White and G. W. Briggs.

The Chairman of the Pleshey Retreat House Committee.

The S.P.G.

The S.C.M. Press—*Student Prayer* and *Prayers New and Old.*

Lady Sykes—a prayer by Percy Dearmer.

Mrs Temple—a prayer by Archbishop William Temple.

The World Council of Churches.

Preface

The first edition of *Acts of Devotion*, compiled by F. W. Dwelly, the then Dean of Liverpool, and published in 1928, was a godsend in providing suitable devotions for use after the third collect, for special occasions, and for gatherings in which a short act of worship was needed.

In thirty-five years, however, times have changed. The new knowledge of the universe has enlarged our faith in God as Creator; the destruction of the second world war and the immense power in the hands of men have emphasized man's need of redemption; the relationship between nations, the division between East and West, the emancipation of nations in Asia and Africa, underline the need of world community. People move about the world much more frequently and much more quickly than ever before. What happens in one country affects almost every other country. News travels round the world in a matter of seconds. We begin to see that we are indeed members one of another.

All this affects our thinking and our mode of expression. The first edition of *Acts of Devotion* reflected the climate of opinion and the idiom of expression of the time when it was compiled. This completely new edition tries to be relevant to conditions to-day, yet at the same time to be an expression of an unchanging faith. To the compiler the rule of faith is the need of prayer, and the litanies and prayers that he has brought together are as much an expression of faith in God's unchanging love and wisdom as they are of man's changing need. They follow the human conditions of man's life, as well as the circumstances in which he has to live that life.

It is the compiler's hope that this new edition will meet the needs of faith and devotion to-day, with an inspiration akin to that of the original edition.

God at Work

Let us try to see God as Creator of the universe, in the galaxies of stars, in the immensities of space, in the tiny and perfect things, wonderful and lovely under the microscope, in the marvels of energy.

> Lord, I believe:
> *Help thou mine unbelief.*

Let us see God at work in the development of men and nations, making the world one, drawing all men to live together as a family.

> Lord, I believe:
> *Help thou mine unbelief.*

Let us assert our trust in God in the problems of pain and catastrophe, believing that he is love, ever willing the true happiness of men.

> Lord, I believe:
> *Help thou mine unbelief.*

Let us seek him at work in the secret souls of men, and praise him for his guidance, so often unrecognized.

> Lord, I believe:
> *Help thou mine unbelief.*

Let us see God at work in the revival of the other religions, focusing men's attention in the spiritual and eternal, gathering all men and all truth into Christ Jesus.

> Lord, I believe:
> *Help thou mine unbelief.*

Let us thank God for the growing concern about the increase of crime and the fall in moral standards, bringing home to men their need of faith in a God of holiness and love.

> Lord, I believe:
> *Help thou mine unbelief.*

Let us praise God for the lightening of men's labours, giving them time for leisure, for fellowship with one another and for the enjoyment of lovely things.

> Lord, I believe:
> *Help thou mine unbelief.*

Let us praise God that our souls are restless until we find our peace in him.

> Lord, I believe:
> *Help thou mine unbelief.*

Let us hold fast our faith in the Church, the people of God, the Body of his Christ, the loving community, the pattern for the life of mankind.

> Lord, I believe:
> *Help thou mine unbelief.*

Let us be bold to offer ourselves lovingly and humbly to assist him in all his purposes.

> Our Father . . .
> *but deliver us from evil.*

O the depth of the riches of the wisdom and knowledge of God! How unsearchable are his judgements, and his ways past finding out!

> *For of him,*
> *and through him,*
> *and to him are all things:*
> *To whom be glory for ever. Amen.*

Thanksgiving for Jesus Christ

Almighty God, Father of our Lord Jesus Christ, we thine unworthy servants do give thee most humble and hearty thanks for all thy goodness and loving kindness to us and to all men. And above all for thine inestimable love in the redemption of the world by our Lord Jesus Christ.

For his humble birth at Bethlehem:
Most humble thanks, O God.

For the taking of our nature
Most humble thanks, O God.

For the obedience of Nazareth
Most humble thanks, O God.

For his identification with sinful men
at his baptism
Most humble thanks, O God.

For the search for thy will in the
forty days of prayer
Most humble thanks, O God.

For the simplicity and depth of his teaching
Most hearty thanks, O God.

For his compassion on the suffering
Most hearty thanks, O God.

And his forgiveness of sinners
Most hearty thanks, O God.

For the defencelessness of the Cross
Most hearty thanks, O God.

For the triumph of the resurrection
We bless thee, O God.

And the glory of the ascension
We bless thee, O God.

For his perpetual prayer for us in heaven
We bless thee, O God.

And for the sending of the Holy Spirit
We bless thee, O God.

Blessed be the Lord God of Israel:
For he hath visited and redeemed his people.
And hath raised up a mighty salvation for us:
In the house of his servant David.
To give knowledge of salvation unto his people:
For the remission of their sins.
Through the tender mercy of our God:
*Whereby the dayspring from on high hath visited **us**.*

All:

To thy Name, Lord Jesus
   help me to bow the knee
      and all its worshipping;
   bow the head
      and all its thinking;
   bow the will
      and all its choosing;
   bow the heart
      and all its loving;
   to-day, to-morrow,
      and all the days of my life.

To the Holy Spirit

O Spirit of God, brooding over the formless world:
brood over my spirit.
> *Blest Holy Spirit.*

O Spirit of God, giving form to the formless: fashion
my spirit.
> *Blest Holy Spirit.*

O Spirit of God, bringing order out of chaos: order
my spirit.
> *Blest Holy Spirit.*

O Spirit of God, giving life to the lifeless: give life to
my spirit.
> *Blest Holy Spirit.*

O Spirit of the Lord, inspiration of the prophets:
speak to my spirit.
> *Blest Holy Spirit.*

O Holy Spirit, Author of holiness: sanctify my spirit.
> *Blest Holy Spirit.*

O Holy Spirit, knowing the deep things of God: move
in the depths of my being.
> *Blest Holy Spirit.*

Fire of the Spirit! Burn all that is not holy.
> *Blest Holy Spirit.*

Fire of the Spirit! Shine with thy light.
> *Blest Holy Spirit.*

Fire of the Spirit! Kindle with thy warmth.
> *Blest Holy Spirit.*

Fire of the Spirit! Generate in us power.
Blest Holy Spirit.

Fire of the Spirit! Inflame us with love.
Blest Holy Spirit.

Wind of the Spirit! Breathe in us thy gentleness.
Blest Holy Spirit.

Wind of the Spirit! Blow in thy strength.
Blest Holy Spirit.

Let us pray for the gift of the Spirit.

The gift of the Spirit is wisdom and understanding, resourcefulness and spiritual strength, knowledge and true godliness, and holy fear. Grant us thy sevenfold gift, O Holy Spirit.
Blest Holy Spirit.

Let us pray for the fruit of the Spirit.

The harvest of the Spirit is love, joy, peace, good temper, gentleness, goodness, humility and self-control. Produce in us thy harvest, O Holy Spirit.
Blest Holy Spirit.

O Holy Spirit,
   Giver of light and life,
impart to us thoughts higher than our own thoughts
   and prayers better than our own prayers,
   and powers beyond our own powers,
that we may spend and be spent
in the ways of love and goodness,
                    after the perfect image
of our Lord and Saviour Jesus Christ.
                    Amen.

Benedicite

I

Let us give thanks to God for the beauty of the world:

For light and darkness, sunrise and sunset, morning
and evening:
Praise him and magnify him for ever.

For the light and warmth of the sun and the beauty
of the moon and stars:
Praise him and magnify him for ever.

For the strength of mountains and hills, and for the
quiet of valleys:
Praise him and magnify him for ever.

For the beauty of water, still or in motion, for streams
and rivers, lakes and seas:
Praise him and magnify him for ever.

For the wind, in its gentleness or strength, in the
rustling of leaves and corn:
Praise him and magnify him for ever.

For flowers of hedgerow, field, and garden:
Praise him and magnify him for ever.

For trees; in the bareness of winter, in the fresh life of
spring, in the shade of summer, and in the colours of
autumn:
Praise him and magnify him for ever.

For the perfection of tiny insects, the playfulness of the small creatures, the friendliness of animals living close to men and the wonder of those in forest and bush:
> *Praise him and magnify him for ever.*

For the birds in their endless variety, in the sweetness of their song and in the mystery of their flight:
> *Praise him and magnify him for ever.*

For vegetables and corn and for the fruits in their season:
> *Praise him and magnify him for ever.*

O all ye works of the Lord, bless ye the Lord:
> *Praise him and magnify him for ever.*

O ye children of men, bless ye the Lord:
> *Praise him and magnify him for ever.*

Grant, O Lord, we pray thee, that as we look upon the beauty of the world, our hearts may be lifted to thee, who art more lovely than the things thou hast created, the First Author of all beauty, who hast prepared for them that love thee the vision of thy eternal loveliness, through Jesus Christ our Lord. *Amen.*

II

Let us give thanks to God for our own creation:

> I am fearfully and wonderfully made:
> And that my soul knoweth right well.

For my birth and life:
> *I praise thee, O God.*

For the strength of my body, its resistance to disease, and its power of recovery:
> *I praise thee, O God.*

For the workings of my hands:
> *I praise thee, O God.*

For the journeyings of my feet:
> *I praise thee, O God.*

For the seeing of my eyes and the hearing of my ears:
> *I praise thee, O God.*

For the sight of beauty in nature and in art:
> *I praise thee, O God.*

For the interest and joy of reading:
> *I praise thee, O God.*

For the meaning and beauty of words:
> *I praise thee, O God.*

And the melodies and harmonies of music:
> *I praise thee, O God.*

For the efficient working of my brain:
> *I praise thee, O God.*

For the power of mind and thought:
> *I praise thee, O God.*

For the sensitiveness and strength of feeling:
> *I praise thee, O God.*

For the sense of conscience:
> *I praise thee, O God.*

For the gift of will:
> *I praise thee, O God.*

For my inner self, its hidden nature, its name known only to thee:
> *I praise thee, O God.*

For its need of thee, its consciousness of thee, its communion with thee:
> *I praise thee, O God.*

For its hope of eternal life, through thy Son Jesus Christ:
> *I praise thee, O God.*

III

O all ye works of the Lord, bless ye the Lord:
> *Praise him and magnify him for ever.*

O ye angels of the Lord, bless ye the Lord:
> *Praise him and magnify him for ever.*

O ye children of men, bless ye the Lord:
> *Praise him and magnify him for ever.*

O ye people of God, bless ye the Lord:
> *Praise him and magnify him for ever.*

O ye priests of the Lord, bless ye the Lord:
> *Praise him and magnify him for ever.*

O ye servants of the Lord, bless ye the Lord:
> *Praise him and magnify him for ever.*

O ye spirits and souls of the righteous, bless ye the Lord:
> *Praise him and magnify him for ever.*

O ye holy and humble men of heart, bless ye the Lord:
>*Praise him and magnify him for ever.*

O ye my friends, bless ye the Lord:
>*Praise him and magnify him for ever.*

Bless the Lord, O my soul, and all that is within me:
>*Praise him and magnify him for ever.*

For the Church

We thank thee, O God, for the Church, the Body of
thy Son, the community of those who believe in him
and commit themselves to him, so that he may com-
plete the work begun in his incarnate life:
> *We praise thee, O God.*

We pray thee that the Church may be as a city set on
a hill and that her light may shine forth in all the dark
places of the World:
> *We pray thee, O God.*

That the Church may be one with the unity which
Christ wills, brought about in the way which he
himself shall choose:
> *We pray thee, O God.*

That all her members may be deepened in penitence
for the sin of disunity, which hinders her mission and
delays men from seeing their Lord and Saviour:
> *We pray thee, O God.*

That the Church may be holy in all her members, in
all her branches and in every congregation:
> *We pray thee, O God.*

That the Church may be truly catholic, for all men,
of every race, in every generation, and catholic in the
fullness of truth:
> *We pray thee, O God.*

That the Church may be apostolic, knowing that
mission is the very essence of her nature, living in the
spirit of the first apostles and in their faith:
> *We pray thee, O God.*

That the Church may have the wisdom of the Spirit to present the Gospel so that men may understand, and see in it good news in their own situation:
We pray thee, O God.

That in the encounter with men of other faiths the Church may present her Lord as the fulfiller of all that is true and the corrector of all that is false:
We pray thee, O God.

That the Church may gladly recognise truth, goodness, and love wherever they are found, and praise thee for the work of thy Eternal Word:
We pray thee, O God.

That the Church may have such a compassion and love for men, that they may be drawn to thee the Author of love and mercy:
We pray thee, O God.

That each local church may be a centre of true worship, a source of grace, a community of love, a fellowship of witness, loving concern and service:
We pray thee, O God.

That thy Church may be so faithful to her Lord, that her life may be the pattern for the life of the world:
We pray thee, O God.

Almighty God, whose Son Jesus Christ came to cast fire upon the earth: grant that by the prayers of thy faithful people a fire of burning zeal may be kindled and pass from heart to heart, that the light of thy Church may shine forth bright and clear to all mankind; through the same thy Son Jesus Christ our Lord. *Amen.*

For the Whole State of Christ's Church

Let us beseech the all-holy and ever-blessed Trinity to send forth mercy and grace upon us and upon all people.

> O God the Father, have mercy upon us:
> *O God the Father, have mercy upon us.*
> O God the Son, have mercy upon us:
> *O God the Son, have mercy upon us.*
> O God the Holy Ghost, have mercy upon us:
> *O God the Holy Ghost, have mercy upon us.*

Stretch out thy hand upon us, O Lord, and save us; raise us up and defend us:
> *Lord, have mercy.*

Let us pray for the peace that cometh from above, and for the salvation of our souls:
> *Lord, have mercy.*

Let us pray for the peace of the whole world, and for the welfare and unity of the Church of God:
> *Lord, have mercy.*

Let us pray for the conversion of those in unbelief and error:
> *Lord, have mercy.*

Let us pray for our country, for this place (*or* city), for this diocese, and for all that dwell therein:
> *Lord, have mercy.*

Let us pray for all Christian people throughout the world:
> *Lord, have mercy.*

Let us pray for all Christian princes and rulers:
Lord, have mercy.

Let us pray for all in authority in this land, especially those in this county (*or* city *or* place):
Lord, have mercy.

Let us pray for the bishops and clergy of Christ's Church, especially for N. our Bishop:
Lord, have mercy.

Let us pray for all voyagers and travellers:
Lord, have mercy.

Let us pray for steadfastness in the Faith for our brethren beyond the seas:
Lord, have mercy.

Let us pray for all who are sick or suffering, in mind, body, or estate:
Lord, have mercy.

Let us pray for a holy and happy death, for rest in paradise, and for the perfect vision of the glory of God:
Lord, have mercy.

Let us pray that we may follow the blessed saints and martyrs in bearing our cross before the world:
Lord, have mercy.

Let us pray for the faithful departed:
Lord, have mercy.

O God of unchangeable power and eternal light, look favourably on thy whole Church, that wonderful and sacred mystery; and by the tranquil operation of thy perpetual providence carry out the work of man's salvation; and let the whole world feel and see that things which were cast down are being raised up, and things which had grown old are being made new, and all things are returning to perfection through him from whom they took their origin, even Jesus Christ our Lord. *Amen.*

For the World Mission of the Church

O God, our Father, by whom the whole family in heaven and earth is made one, who revealest thyself in Jesus Christ, who givest peace through thy Holy Spirit:
> *Hear us, we pray.*

As we hear the commission which thou hast given to thy Church and search for that power which thou hast promised to all who know Christ as Lord:
> *Hear us, we pray.*

As we pray for thy help in our searching after renewed life and holy unity, and in our response to thy Spirit which would be known in all the world:
> *Hear us, we pray.*

That it may please thee to strengthen and enlarge thy Holy Church in every land, and to unite those who profess and call themselves Christians in faith, hope, love, and action:
> *We beseech thee, good Lord.*

That thy Church may strive, not for its own safety, but for the world's salvation, seeking only thy Kingdom and thy righteousness:
> *We beseech thee, good Lord.*

That thy Church may proclaim the Gospel throughout the earth, and bring all men to obedience in thee:
> *We beseech thee, good Lord.*

That thy sons, knowing in thy Church a life unbroken by differences of nation, race, or class, may dare to witness to this life in the world about them:
> *We beseech thee, good Lord.*

By thy ministry of healing and forgiveness, by thy gift of salvation, by thy gifts of renewal through which our tired world may grow young again:

Hasten thy Kingdom, good Lord.

By thy inspiration of human skill through which the words of science, art, and letters come to express thy glory; by thy strengthening of the prophets that they may be the forerunners of thy Kingdom:

Hasten thy Kingdom, good Lord.

By thy gift of life to the Church that it may have courage to go forward; by the establishing of thy justice among men and thy rule over social and industrial life:

Hasten thy Kingdom, good Lord.

By thy love shown in Christ's crucifixion, the power of his resurrection and the inspiration of thy Sacraments:

Hasten thy Kingdom, good Lord.

For thy Church Universal, for its vision vouchsafed unto us, and for the gracious gift of this fellowship:

We praise thee, we bless thee, we magnify thee,
O Lord most High.   Amen.

For Church and Nation

O God the Father, God of all righteousness, make us a righteous nation:
> *We humbly pray.*

O God the Son, Redeemer of all mankind, make us a redeemed people:
> *We humbly pray.*

O God the Spirit, Lord of all holiness, make us a holy Church:
> *We humbly pray.*

O Holy, Blessed, and Glorious Trinity, draw us into thy eternal love:
> *We humbly pray.*

Remember not, O Lord, our sins, nor the sins of our Church and nation:
> *Cleanse us, Holy Lord.*

From selfishness, from love of ease and pleasure and from indifference to the needs of others:
> *Cleanse us, Holy Lord.*

From prejudice of race, colour and class, from party spirit and from slavery to the opinion of others:
> *Cleanse us, Holy Lord.*

From national pride and greed, from indifference to the needs and problems of other nations, and from failure to judge our own nation by the standards of thy Kingdom:
> *Cleanse us, Holy Lord.*

We pray thee to hear us, Holy Lord; and that it may please thee to bless the Catholic Church and to set it ablaze with the fire of thy Spirit:
Hear us, Holy Lord.

That thy Church may be as the salt of the earth, saving our nation from corruption, preserving it in righteousness and giving it true character and life:
Hear us, Holy Lord.

That all who believe in thee may be of one heart and soul, striving for thy Kingdom among men:
Hear us, Holy Lord.

That there may never fail a succession of prophets of vision and power, and priests of holiness and love:
Hear us, Holy Lord.

That it may please thee to bless all Christian rulers, and to bless our leaders with wisdom, courage, and integrity:
Hear us, Holy Lord.

That all who work in commerce and industry may provide things of true value, and all who work in offices, shops, and factories may render good work and honest service:
Hear us, Holy Lord.

That it may please thee to strengthen all unions of workers and employers to work together for the welfare of their industries and for the common good:
Hear us, Holy Lord.

That it may please thee to bless all who form and guide public opinion, all statesmen and politicians, all preachers and speakers, all editors and writers, all journalists and broadcasters:
Hear us, Holy Lord.

That, in an age of comfort and plenty, we may be guarded against materialism and worldliness, and forgetfulness of the deep needs of the human spirit:

Hear us, Holy Lord.

That it may please thee to sanctify our family life with discipline in sex and faithfulness in marriage, to grant us understanding of the young, and love for the old, the lonely, and those who find themselves inadequate to the demands of life:

Hear us, Holy Lord.

O Lord Christ, who for the world's sake didst stand against the world: Grant that thy Church may stand for the world against the world, and love the world with something of thy great love, for the world's sake. *Amen.*

O Father of the just, do thou of thine infinite goodness direct the hearts of all who bear authority. Help them with the power of thy Holy Spirit to make laws in accordance with thy will, and for the advancement of righteousness. Protect them from the snares of the enemy and the deceits of the world; let no pride of power betray them into rejection of thy commandments; and grant that both rulers and people may with one mind serve thee our God and King, through Jesus Christ. *Amen.*

For the Unity of the Church

Let us remember
the unity which God himself has given us:
One body, one Spirit, one hope of our calling:
One Lord, one faith, one baptism
One God and Father of all
Over all, through all,
in all.

Glory be to thee, O Lord.

Let us pray
with our Lord the prayers he prayed
on the night before he died on the Cross

Sanctify us in thy truth—not in expediency, compromise or human ingenuity, but in truth, thy truth.
Holy Father, make us one.

Keep us in thy Name—true to the revelation of thyself in Jesus Christ.
Holy Father, make us one.

Keep us from the evil one—so clever at disguising our partisanship, so quick to divide.
Holy Father, make us one.

Make us one—with the unity within thine own Being, surpassing any unity we know.
Holy Father, make us one.

That the world may believe—lest the conversion of the world and the salvation of men be hindered and delayed.
Holy Father, make us one.

O Lord Christ, our great High Priest, whose prayers and promises were not for thy apostles only, but for all those who should believe on thee by their word unto the world's end: Breathe upon us thy holy and glorious Spirit, to knit us to thyself and to one another in an indestructible bond; as thou and the Father are one in the unity of the same Spirit, God, for ever and ever. *Amen.*

Let us pray

that the Lord of the Church
will grant to the Church the unity that is his will
and in the way that he himself shall choose.

O Lord of the Church, make the Church one, and heal our divisions:
> *O Lord of the Church.*

O Lord of the Church, make the Church holy, in all her members and in all her branches:
> *O Lord of the Church.*

O Lord of the Church, make the Church catholic, for all men and in all truth:
> *O Lord of the Church.*

O Lord of the Church, make the Church apostolic, with the faith and mission of the first apostles:
> *O Lord of the Church.*

A PRAYER FOR RENEWAL

Spirit of promise, Spirit of unity, we thank thee that thou art also the Spirit of renewal. Renew in the whole Church, we pray thee, that passionate desire for the coming of thy Kingdom which will unite all Christians in one mission to the world. May we grow up together into him who is our Head, the Saviour of the world, and our only Lord and Master. *Amen.*

A PRAYER OF TRUST

Into thy hands, our Father, we commit this thy world, this thy family, for which our Lord Jesus Christ was content to be betrayed, and to suffer death upon the cross. Into thy hands we commit thy Universal Church and her unity. Into thy hands we commit all the problems which seem insoluble, in sure and certain hope; for in thee is our trust. Here and now we lay all in thy hands. All Love, all Glory, be unto thee for ever and ever.

For our Parish Church

I

Here, O Lord, let thy priests be clothed with righteousness and let thy saints sing with joyfulness:
> *In this house, O Lord.*

Here let thy priests offer the sacrifice of praise and thanksgivings, and thy people pay their vows unto the most Highest:
> *In this house, O Lord.*

Here let them offer their free-will offerings, with a holy worship:
> *In this house, O Lord.*

Here let the burden of sin be loosed, and broken and contrite hearts be healed:
> *In this house, O Lord.*

Here let thy servants find support in their trials, and a refuge in their distress:
> *In this house, O Lord.*

Here let thy holy Name be for ever worshipped and adored, through thy Son our Saviour Jesus Christ:
> *Amen.*

II

Father, we pray thee to fill this house with thy Spirit:
> *Father, we pray thee.*

Here may the strong renew their strength and seek for their waking hours a noble consecration:

Father, we pray thee.

Here may the poor find succour and the friendless friendship:

Father, we pray thee.

Here may the tempted find power, the sorrowing comfort, and the bereaved find the truth that death hath no dominion over their beloved:

Father, we pray thee.

Here let the fearing find a new courage and the doubting have their faith and hope confirmed:

Father, we pray thee.

Here may the careless be awakened and all that are oppressed be freed:

Father, we pray thee.

Hither may many be drawn by thy love and go hence, their doubts resolved and faith renewed, their fears at rest, their courage high, their purpose firm, their sins forgiven, and their hearts aflame with thy love:

Father, we pray thee

through Jesus Christ our Lord.   *Amen.*

O Lord Jesus Christ, who art thyself the temple of the holy City of God, the light thereof and its surpassing glory: glorify and lighten, we beseech thee, with thy perpetual presence this earthly house built gloriously to thee; and be pleased both to inspire and to accept its worship day by day, the praise of thankful lips and the prayers of faithful hearts; who livest and reignest with the Father and the Holy Ghost, one God, for ever and ever.

O Lord Jesus Christ, who didst go, as thy custom was, into the synagogue on the sabbath day; Quicken with thy abiding presence the life of thy Church in our country; that every church may be as a city set upon a hill, a witness to thy claims upon our worship and service, a power-house of prayer, a community of love, and a joy and comfort to thy servants. Hear us from thy throne in heaven, where with the Father and the Holy Spirit thou livest and reignest, one God, world without end.

Each in his own Ministry

All thy works praise thee, O Lord:
And thy saints give thanks unto thee.
They show the glory of thy Kingdom:
And talk of thy power.
That thy power, thy glory and
the mightiness of thy Kingdom:
Might be known unto men.

Let us pray.

O God, we pray thee for thy Church, which is set to-day amid the challenges of new knowledge and the perplexities of a changing order, and is face to face with a new task. Fill us all afresh with the Spirit of Pentecost. Help us to proclaim boldly and persuasively the coming of thy Kingdom in terms which men can understand and which will bring new light to their minds and fresh grace to their lives; through him who makes all things new, even Jesus Christ our Lord and Master. *Amen.*

We thank thee
O God

That in Jesus Christ thou didst incarnate thyself in human nature and didst speak to us in terms of our own life in the world:
We thank thee, Eternal God.

That thy Son founded the Church to continue his creative and reconciling work:
We thank thee, Eternal God.

For his teaching that the Church is to be as salt in the world, cleansing and preserving it through the sacrifice of itself:

> *We thank thee, Eternal God.*

For his promise that the gates of hell shall not prevail, either in repelling the forces of thy Kingdom or in retaining the prisoners of evil:

> *We thank thee, Eternal God.*

For the presence of the Holy Spirit to recall us to the remembrance of our Lord and to interpret his teaching to every age and situation:

> *We thank thee, Eternal God.*

For the realization that the Church is, as it was in the beginning, a revolutionary movement in every man's life and in every situation:

> *We thank thee, Eternal God.*

Let us pray

That we may put ourselves alongside our fellow men and see the Christian faith and life from their point of view:

> *Lord, hear our prayer.*

That the Church may be aware of the rapid rate of change both in the thought of men and in their social circumstances:

> *Lord, hear our prayer.*

For the wisdom of the Holy Spirit in the large-scale and complex problems of society and work to-day, which require corporate judgements and solutions:

> *Lord, hear our prayer.*

That in the choices facing mankind to-day in situations partly good and partly evil, we may be granted the insights of the Holy Spirit, and guided to make decisions which will forward thy will:

> *Lord, hear our prayer.*

That thou wilt grant to Christians working in big organizations the faith that they can share in some small way thy active concern for the good ordering of men's lives and the supply of their needs:

Lord, hear our prayer.

That we may see in our daily work the opportunity for serving thee by the truth of our insights, the honesty of our service, and the concern for our fellow-workers:

Lord, hear our prayer.

That thou wilt bless those groups of Christians who are trying to discover how they may best exercise Christian vocation through their professions:

Lord, hear our prayer.

That our local churches may no longer be seen as arks of safety, but as power-houses of grace for the invading forces of thy Kingdom:

Lord, hear our prayer.

That thou wilt bless and guide all lay movements which seek to advance thy Kingdom in special spheres of work or in particular neighbourhoods:

Lord, hear our prayer.

That thou wilt guide our local churches to face the challenge of such movements, to learn from them and to offer understanding and grateful fellowship:

Lord, hear our prayer.

That thou wilt enable the clergy to bring the light of thy truth to their people and the grace of the Sacraments to their strengthening:

Lord, hear our prayer.

Let us sum up our praises and prayers saying together:

Almighty and everlasting God,
by whose spirit the whole body of the Church
is governed and sanctified:

Receive our supplications and prayers
which we offer before thee
for all estates of men in thy holy Church,
that every member of the same,
in his vocation and ministry,
may truly and godly serve thee;
through our Lord and Saviour Jesus Christ.
Amen.

Now unto him that is able to stablish you according to the Gospel of Jesus Christ, made known unto all the nations, for their obedience to the faith, to the only wise God be the glory for ever and ever. *Amen.*

For all in Education

Let us offer to Almighty God through our Lord Jesus Christ our thanks for all the benefits that we ourselves have received from those who taught and guided us, and from the schools and colleges in which we were once pupils:

Thanks be to God.

For God's gift to man of memory, of understanding and reason, of imagination, of the hunger for truth:

Thanks be to God.

For the revelation of God our Father, his truth and love, in his incarnate Son, and for all the gifts of light and life through his Holy Spirit:

Thanks be to God.

For God's calling of men to minister knowledge to the children of men:

Thanks be to God.

For our universities, colleges, and schools, and the increasing value set upon the right education of the young:

Thanks be to God.

For all benefactors to sound learning and research remembered or forgotten; and for the many benefits which we owe to their bounty, let us bless the Lord:

Thanks be to God.

For all who are called to the ministry of teaching, let us bless the Lord:

Thanks be to God.

We pray

For all boys and girls at school, that while they grow in knowledge they may also grow in grace: and learning to love thee, may learn for thy sake to love and serve their fellow-men:
We pray thee to hear us, O Lord.

We pray for all students, especially for those who are learning to be teachers, that setting before themselves the pattern of thy Son, our Lord Jesus Christ, they may fitly prepare themselves for their life's work:
We pray thee to hear us, O Lord.

We pray for all parents, that they may guide, encourage and care for their children as they might:
We pray thee to hear us, O Lord.

We pray for all teachers, that they may do their work with wisdom, vigour and devotion; that they may understand and love the children committed to their care; that they may find in thee power and inspiration according to their need:
We pray thee to hear us, O Lord.

We pray for all places of learning, especially . . . . . , that thy blessing may rest upon them; that all who work in them may be knit together in friendship and a common sincerity; that all may be done for thy glory and the true benefit of thy children:
We pray thee to hear us, O Lord.

All:

Eternal Light, shine into our hearts,
Eternal Goodness, deliver our thoughts from evil,
Eternal Power, support our prayer,
Eternal Wisdom, scatter the darkness of our ignorance,
Eternal Pity, have mercy upon us;
That with all our heart and mind and soul and strength we may seek thy face, and be brought by thine infinite mercy to thy holy presence; through Jesus Christ our Lord.

For the Peace of the World

We believe in God the Father, who calls all men to be his children:

> *We believe.*

We believe in God the Son, who brings forgiveness to all men:

> *We believe.*

We believe in God the Spirit, whose will it is to live in all men:

> *We believe.*

We believe that God wills peace on earth, among men of goodwill:

> *We believe.*

We believe that it is God's will that all men should have abundant life:

> *We believe.*

We believe that it is God's will that we should bear one another's burdens:

> *We believe.*

We believe that it is God's will to establish his rule among men:

> *We believe.*

We believe that it is God's will to gather all men into one in Jesus Christ:

> *We believe.*

All:

Our Father,
*   Who art in heaven:*
*   Hallowed be thy Name,*
*   Thy Kingdom come,*
*   Thy Will be done*
in earth as it is in heaven.   Amen.

Let us pray

FOR PEACE

Grant, O Lord, to the nations wisdom to understand the things that belong unto peace and the will to reject the things that make for division and war. Grant that realizing our common humanity we may live together as a family, and make the world a home, bearing one another's burdens, ministering to one another's needs, obeying thy laws of righteousness and acknowledging thee to be the God and Father of us all, who hast made us thy children in Jesus Christ our Lord.

FOR ALL IN AUTHORITY

O Father of the just, do thou of thine infinite goodness direct the hearts of all who bear authority. Help them with the power of thy Holy Spirit to make laws in accordance with thy will, and for the advancement of righteousness. Protect them from the snares of the enemy and the deceits of the world; let no pride of power betray them into rejection of thy commandments; and grant that both rulers and people may with one mind serve thee our God and King, through Jesus Christ.

FOR THE RIGHT USE OF POWER

Almighty and merciful God, without whom all things hasten to destruction and fall into nothingness: Look, we beseech thee, upon thy family of nations and men, to which thou hast committed power in trust for their mutual health and comfort. Save us and help us, O Lord, lest we abuse thy gift and make it our misery and ruin; draw all men unto thee in thy Kingdom of righteousness and truth; uproot our enmities, heal our divisions, cast out our fears; and renew our faith in thine unchanging purpose of goodwill and peace on earth; for the love of Jesus Christ our Lord.

FOR THE COMING OF THE KINGDOM

O Lord, who hast set before us thy great hope that thy Kingdom shall come, and hast taught us to pray for its coming: give us grace to discern the signs of its dawning, and to work for the perfect day when thy will shall be done on earth as it is in heaven; through Jesus Christ our Lord.

Let us dedicate ourselves to work for peace—in our homes, in our own country and among the nations—saying together a prayer of St Francis of Assisi:

> All:
> *Lord, make us instruments of thy peace,*
> *Where there is hatred, let us sow love;*
> *Where there is injury, pardon;*
> *Where there is discord, union;*
> *Where there is doubt, faith;*
> *Where there is despair, hope;*
> *Where there is darkness, light;*
> *Where there is sadness, joy;*
> *For thy mercy and thy truth's sake.*
> *Amen.*

May the God of peace give peace in your hearts, peace in your homes, and peace among men, now and always. *Amen.*

For the Sick

O Lord God, we thank thee that all things work together for good, to them who love thee and seek thy will:
> *Lord God, we thank thee.*

O Lord God, we thank thee that in all that happens we are more than conquerors, through him that loves us:
> *Lord God, we thank thee.*

O Lord God, we thank thee that nothing can separate us from thy love, which is in Christ Jesus our Lord:
> *Lord God, we thank thee.*

FOR ALL IN PAIN

Grant, O Lord, to all those who are bearing pain, thy spirit of healing, thy spirit of peace and hope, of courage and endurance. Cast out from them the spirit of anxiety and fear; grant them perfect confidence and trust in thee, that in thy light they may see light; through Jesus Christ our Lord. *Amen.*

FOR THE HALLOWING OF SUFFERING

O Lord, we pray thee for all who are weighed down with the mystery of suffering. Reveal thyself to them as the God of love who thyself dost bear all our sufferings. Grant that they may know that suffering borne in fellowship with thee is not waste or frustration, but can be turned to goodness and blessing, something greater than if they had never suffered, through him who on the Cross suffered rejection and hatred, loneliness and despair, agonizing pain and physical death, and rose victorious from the dead, conquering and to conquer, even Jesus Christ our Lord. *Amen.*

FOR THE SICK IN MIND

O Holy Spirit, who dost search out all things, even the deep things of God and the deep things of man: We pray thee so to penetrate into the springs of personality of all who are sick in mind, to bring them cleansing, healing, and unity. Sanctify all memory, dispel all fear, and bring them to love thee with all their mind and will, that they may be made whole and glorify thee for ever. We ask this in the Name of him who cast out devils and healed men's minds, even Jesus Christ our Lord. *Amen.*

FOR THE HEALING CHURCH

O Lord and Master Jesus Christ, Word of the everlasting Father, who hast borne our griefs and carried the burden of our infirmities: Renew by thy Holy Spirit in thy Church, we beseech thee, thy gifts of healing, and send forth thy disciples again to preach the gospel of thy Kingdom, and to cure the sick and relieve thy suffering children, to the praise and glory of thy holy Name. *Amen.*

FOR ALL WHO SUFFER FROM DISEASES AT PRESENT INCURABLE

O heavenly Father, we pray thee for those suffering from diseases for which at present there is no cure. Give them the victory of trust and hope, that they may never lose their faith in Thy loving purpose. Grant thy wisdom to all who are working to discover the causes of disease, and the realization that through Thee all things are possible. We ask this in the Name of him who went about doing good and healing all manner of disease, even thy Son Jesus Christ our Lord. *Amen.*

O Lord Jesus Christ, who in thy last agony didst commend thy spirit into the hands of thy heavenly Father: have mercy upon all sick and dying persons; may death be unto them the gate of eternal life. Grant them at the last the assurance that, whether we wake or sleep, we are still with thee, who art the resurrection and life of all the faithful, blessed for evermore. *Amen.*

A PRAYER OF BLESSING

May the Father bless them, who created all things in the beginning; may the Son of God heal them; may the Holy Spirit enlighten them, guard their bodies, save their souls, direct their thoughts, and bring them safe to the heavenly country, where Father, Son, and Holy Spirit ever reign, one God blessed for evermore. *Amen.*

For the Departed

Jesus said: I am the resurrection and the life; he that believeth on me, though he die, yet shall he live; and whosoever liveth and believeth on me shall never die.
We praise thee, Lord of life and death.

Whether we live, we live unto the Lord; and whether we die, we die unto the Lord; whether we live therefore, or die, we are the Lord's.
We praise thee, Lord of life and death.

If we believe that Jesus died and rose again, even so them also that are fallen asleep in Jesus will God bring with him.
We praise thee, Lord of life and death.

Father of all, we pray to thee for those whom we love but see no longer. Grant them thy peace.
And let light perpetual shine upon them.

Grant unto them the forgiveness of all their sins.
Lord, have mercy upon them.

Grant that they may grow in holiness and love.
Christ, have mercy upon them.

Work in them the good purpose of thy perfect will.
Lord, have mercy upon them.

On all who have died with unforgiven sins:
Lord, have mercy.

On all who have died without the knowledge of thy love:
Lord, have mercy.

On all who died without friends to pray for them:
Lord, have mercy.

Let them dwell in thy house for ever:
For ever and ever.

With all whom they have loved:
For ever and ever.

With the spirits of just men made perfect:
For ever and ever.

With the prophets, saints, and martyrs of every age:
For ever and ever.

With angels and archangels and all the company of heaven:
For ever and ever.

In the presence of thy glory:
For ever and ever. Amen.

For all the Saints

O Eternal Lord God, we thy children lift grateful thanks to thee for our elder brethren in the household of faith:

For Abraham the father of the faithful:
Blessed be thou, Lord God of Israel.

For the patriarchs who succeeded him in faith:
Blessed be thou, Lord God of Israel.

For Moses, who under thee led thy people to freedom and gave them thy law:
Blessed be thou, Lord God of Israel.

For the prophets to whom thy Word came:
Blessed be thou, Lord God of Israel.

For David, the first singer of thy praises:
Blessed be thou, Lord God of Israel.

For those who gave their lives to preserve thy law:
Blessed be thou, Lord God of Israel.

For Jesus, thy Christ, thy Word in person, Mediator of the new covenant, Saviour of men, King of saints:
Praise be to thee, O God, and to thy Christ.

For the first disciples who left all to follow him:
Praise be to thee, O God, and to thy Christ.

For the apostles, who in obedience to him carried the Gospel to many lands:
Praise be to thee, O God, and to thy Christ.

For thy servant Paul, who so richly experienced the grace of the Risen Lord, and interpreted him to the nations:
Praise be to thee, O God, and to thy Christ.

For the evangelists who recorded the apostles' memories of their Lord and their own faith in him:
Praise be to thee, O God, and to thy Christ.

For the messengers, known and unknown, who brought the good news to our own country:
Praise be to thee, O God, and to thy Christ.

For all who have gone to the ends of the earth to share thy love in Christ Jesus:
Praise be to thee, O God, and to thy Christ.

For the noble army of martyrs who faced death for love of thee and in thy power:
Praise be to thee, O King of Saints.

For the saints in every age who reflected thee in their lives and ever since:
Praise be to thee, O King of Saints.

Who stood fast in the faith and worked the works of love:
Praise be to thee, O King of Saints.

For the succession of quiet and gracious souls, whose presence has sweetened and sanctified the world:
Praise be to thee, O King of Saints.

For the mighty company of every race and nation who worship in thy presence:
Praise be to thee, O King of Saints.

O Almighty God, who hast knit together thine elect in one communion and fellowship, in the mystical body of thy Son Christ our Lord: Grant us grace to follow thy blessed saints in all virtuous and godly living, that we may come to those unspeakable joys, which thou hast prepared for them that unfeignedly love thee; through Jesus Christ our Lord. *Amen.*

O Lord, who in every age dost reveal thyself to the childlike and lowly in heart, and from every race dost write names in thy book of life: Give us the simplicity and faith of thy saints, that loving thee above all things, we may be what thou wouldest have us be, and do what thou wouldest have us do. So may we be numbered with thy saints in glory everlasting; through Jesus Christ our Lord.

Amen. Blessing, and glory, and wisdom,
and thanksgiving, and honour, and power, and might
be unto our God for ever and ever.   Amen.

A Litany of Love

God so loved the world, that he gave his only-begotten Son, that whosoever believeth on him should not perish, but have eternal life.
> *Glory be to thee, O Lord.*

God commendeth his love towards us, in that, while we were yet sinners, Christ died for us.
> *Glory be to thee, O Lord.*

The love of God hath been shed abroad in our hearts through the Holy Spirit which was given unto us.
> *Glory be to thee, O Lord.*

Hear the first and great commandment:

Thou shalt love the Lord thy God with all thy heart, and with all thy soul, and with all thy mind, and with all thy strength.
> *Lord, teach us love.*

We love him, because he first loved us.
> *Lord, teach us love.*

Hear the second commandment:

Thou shalt love thy neighbour as thyself.
> *Lord, teach us love.*

Love is very patient, very kind. Love knows no jealousy; love makes no parade, gives itself no airs, is never rude, never selfish, never irritated, never resentful.
> *Lord, teach us love.*

Love is never glad when others go wrong, love is gladdened by goodness, always slow to expose, always eager to believe the best, always hopeful, always patient. Love never disappears.

Lord, teach us love.

Hear the new commandment:

A new commandment give I unto you, that ye love one another; even as I have loved you, that ye also love one another.

Lord, teach us love.

We know that we have passed out of death into life, when we love the brethren.

Lord, teach us love.

Beloved, let us love one another; for love is of God; and everyone that loveth is begotten of God, and knoweth God.

Lord, teach us love.

Give us grace, O God our Father, to keep this day and always the new commandment and the great commandment and all the commandments, by loving thee with all our mind and soul and strength, and one another for thy sake; in the Name of Jesus Christ our Lord. *Amen.*

The Disciple's Litany

Jesus meek and humble of heart
           Hear me.

    From the love of being esteemed:
        Deliver me, Jesus.

    From the desire of being loved:
        Deliver me, Jesus.

    From the desire of being sought after:
        Deliver me, Jesus.

    From the desire of being honoured:
        Deliver me, Jesus.

    From the desire of being praised:
        Deliver me, Jesus.

    From the desire of being preferred to others:
        Deliver me, Jesus.

    From the desire of being consulted:
        Deliver me, Jesus.

    From the desire of being approved:
        Deliver me, Jesus.

    From the desire of being valued:
        Deliver me, Jesus.

    From the fear of being humbled:
        Deliver me, Jesus.

    From the fear of being despised:
        Deliver me, Jesus.

From the fear of suffering rebuffs:
Deliver me, Jesus.

From the fear of being misunderstood:
Deliver me, Jesus.

From the fear of being forgotten:
Deliver me, Jesus.

From the fear of being ridiculed:
Deliver me, Jesus.

From the fear of being injured:
Deliver me, Jesus.

From the fear of being suspected:
Deliver me, Jesus.

That others may be loved more than I:
Jesus, grant me the grace to wish.

That others may increase in this world's esteem
And I diminish:
Jesus, grant me the grace to wish.

That others may be employed
And I set aside:
Jesus, grant me the grace to wish.

That others may be praised
And I overlooked:
Jesus, grant me the grace to wish.

That others may be preferred
Before me in everything:
Jesus, grant me the grace to wish.

That others may be more holy than I;
That I may be as holy as thou wouldst have me be:
Jesus, grant me the grace to wish.

Acts of Penitence

I

Let us humbly confess to God our sins and failures.

Our forgetfulness of thee:
> *O Lord, forgive.*

Our unkindness to each other:
> *O Lord, forgive.*

Our selfishness and self-will:
> *O Lord, forgive.*

Our dishonesties:
> *O Lord, forgive.*

Our broken promises:
> *O Lord, forgive.*

Our secret sins:
> *O Lord, forgive.*

Our neglect of opportunities for good:
> *O Lord, forgive.*

All:

Grant, we beseech thee, merciful Lord,
to thy faithful people pardon and peace,
that they may be cleansed
from all their sins,
and serve thee with a quiet mind;
through Jesus Christ our Lord.
Amen.

Priest:

May the Almighty and merciful Lord grant unto
you forgiveness of all your sins, time for amendment
of life, and the grace and comfort of the Holy
Spirit. *Amen.*

II

Let us place ourselves in the presence of God, and in
the thought of his holiness, love and perfection, let us
remember our sins:

> Our besetting sins
> > our secret sins
> our sins in thought
> > word
> > deed
> our sins against others
> our sins against God
> > our falling short of his glory for us.

All:

O Lord God,
> *Forgive what we have been,*
> *Amend what we are,*
> *Direct what we shall be;*
> > *For Jesus Christ's sake.*

Let us dedicate ourselves anew to a God-ruled life:

All:

God be in my head
And in my understanding;
God be in my eyes
And in my looking;
God be in my mouth

And in my speaking;
God be in my heart
And in my thinking;
God be at mine end
And at my departing.

III

Let us ask God to shine his light into the dark places of our hearts and confront us with hidden and secret sins:

All that we keep in the dark:
O God, make us see.

(silence)

Our preoccupation with ourselves
O God, make us see.

Our lustful imaginations, our secret ambitions
O God, make us see.

The buried grudge, the half-acknowledged enmity
O God, make us see.

The bitterness of some past loss not yet offered to thee
O God, make us see.

The private comfort to which we cling
O God, make us see.

The fear of failure which saps our initiative
O God, make us see.

The pessimism which is an insult to thy will and power
O God, make us see.

All:

Here and now, O Holy Lord,
we bring our secret sins to thee:
we lie open in thy sight.
Let thy piercing light
be also our healing,
for the sake of him
who both taught us
and brought us
thy forgiveness;
even Jesus Christ our Saviour.
Amen.

Make me a clean heart, O God:
And renew a right spirit within me.
Cast me not away from thy presence:
And take not thy Holy Spirit from me.

O Lord, who in thy light hast made us see ourselves as we really are: Fill us also with hope to see ourselves as we shall be, when thou hast finished thy work in us; through the grace of the same Jesus Christ our Lord. *Amen.*

O give me the comfort of thy help again:
And stablish me with a willing spirit.
O Lord, open thou my lips:
And my mouth shall show forth thy praise.
O Lord, thou hast forgiven all my sins:
And wilt heal all my infirmities.
Praise the Lord, O my soul:
And all that is within me praise his holy Name.

Acts of Dedication

I

I am come to do thy will, O my God:
I delight to do it; thy law is in my heart.

All:

Look upon our lives, O Lord our God.
And make them thine
In the power of thy Holy Spirit:
That we may walk in thy way,
Faithfully believing thy Word,
And faithfully doing thy commandments;
Faithfully worshipping thee,
And faithfully serving our neighbour;
To the furtherance of thy glorious Kingdom;
Through Jesus Christ our Lord.

Remember, O Lord, what thou hast wrought in us, and not what we deserve, and as thou hast called us to thy service, make us worthy of our calling; through Jesus Christ our Lord.
Amen. Amen.

II

Ye are bought with a price:
Therefore glorify God in your body and in your spirit.

All:

I am no longer my own, but thine.
Put me to what thou wilt,
rank me with whom thou wilt;

put me to doing, put me to suffering;
let me be employed for thee, or laid aside for thee;
exalted for thee, or brought low for thee;
let me be full, let me be empty;
let me have all things, let me have nothing;
I freely and heartily yield all things to thy pleasure and
disposal.

And now, O glorious and blessed God,
Father, Son and Holy Spirit,
thou art mine, and I am thine.
    So be it.
And the covenant which I have made on earth,
let it be ratified in heaven.

Go before us, O Lord, in all our doings with thy most gracious favour, and further us with thy continual help; that in all our works, begun, continued, and ended in thee, we may glorify thy holy Name, and finally by thy mercy obtain everlasting life; through Jesus Christ our Lord. *Amen.*

III

Let us offer ourselves to God and the service of men, saying this prayer together:

All:
O God, make us unselfish and generous.
Help us to strive manfully for all that is right.
Make us merciful to all who are broken or bowed down.
Create in us a clean heart.
Build us more and more into the likeness of thy dear
Son.

Teach us the way of peace,
And let us be of them that make peace;
Through the same Jesus Christ our Lord.

Let us pray for God's help:

All:
May the strength of God guide us,
May the power of God preserve us,
May the wisdom of God instruct us,
May the hand of God lead us,
May the shield of God defend us.
    May Christ be with us,
        Christ before us,
        Christ behind us,
        Christ around us,
        Christ within us,
    This day and for evermore.

IV

O my God, thou hast created me: I depend on thee, I worship thee.
    Father, dear Father!

O my God, thou hast made me in thy image: make me like thy Son.
    Father, dear Father!

O my God, thou hast called me to be thy servant: Help me to obey and serve thee.
    Father, dear Father!

O my God, I am a sinner: and thou hast forgiven me.
    Father, dear Father!

O my God, in my baptism thou hast made me thy child.
    Father, dear Father!

And a member of Christ.
    Father, dear Father!

And an inheritor of the Kingdom of Heaven.
    Father, dear Father!

O Christ, thou hast called me friend.
    I will do thy will.

And a fellow-worker for thy Kingdom.
I will do thy will.

O Holy Spirit, thou hast made me thy temple.
I will do thy will.

O my God, thou hast made me partaker of thy divine nature.
I will do thy will.

And an heir of eternal life. to know, love and enjoy thee for ever.
Father, dear Father!

The Lord's Prayer

Our Father:
 God and Father of Jesus Christ,
  whom we know only through thy Son;
 Father of all who have been made thy sons,
  calling all men to be thy children:

 Our Father.

Which art in Heaven:
 Thou art from everlasting.
 In thee all things exist.
  Highest and holiest,
  eternal and perfect.
 To thee we lift our spirits,

 Who art in Heaven.

Hallowed be thy Name:
 May all men know thee as thou art,
  lifting their hearts to thee
  in reverence and love.
 May every tongue confess thy Name,
  for in no other name
  will men find salvation.

 Hallowed be thy Name on earth, as it is in heaven.

Thy kingdom come:
 King in our hearts;
 Lord of our lives:
  bringing every thought
  into captive obedience.
 In our own country,
 in every country,
  the laws of thy kingdom
  accepted and obeyed.

 Thy kingdom come on earth, as it is in heaven.

Thy will be done:
> Thy wise and loving will
> in which is our peace.
> Victory over evil,
> victory over self,
> the banishment of war.
> Men loving in brotherhood
> as children of thine
> serving each other.

Thy will be done on earth, as it is in heaven.

Give us this day our daily bread:
> Fill us with active pity
> for the millions who hunger,
> for the homeless and displaced
> who live without hope,
> for the sick and suffering
> whom thou wouldest heal,
> Food too for the soul,
> the Bread of Life
> without which men faint,
> hungering for thee.

Give all this day their daily bread.

Forgive us our sins:
> Our open crying sins,
> our secret, whispering sins
> which thou alone dost know.
> Our lack of love,
> our falling short of thy glory;

Forgive, as we forgive.

Forgive the selfishness
> entwined with our nature;
> the lack of care for others:
> refusal to be my brother's keeper.
> Our failure to tell good news,
> to bring men home to thee.

Forgive, as we forgive.

Teach us to hate the cruelty of men,
   all lust of power,
   all pride of race,
   all greed of gain,
   sin against the truth,
   resentment and revenge:

   Forgive, as we forgive.

Help us to understand the need of others,
   the wrongs they suffer,
   their need of thy forgiveness.

   Forgive, as we forgive.

And lead us not into temptation:
   Let us not fall back into weakness and sin,
      nor grasp anything which is not thy will.
   Let us not rest content
      or helpless in face of need,
      cowardly in act or speech
      when called to witness
      that we belong to thee.

   Lead us not into temptation.

Deliver us from evil:
   Not overcome by evil
      but answering with good,
      with hope and courage high,
      founded in thee.
   More than conquerors
      through him that loved us.
   Enduring to the end
      as seeing thee, our Lord.

   For thine is the Kingdom,
   the power and the glory, for ever and ever.
                              Amen.

To-day

I

Lord, let me stand to-day—

For whatever is pure and true and just and good:
Lord, let me stand to-day.

For the advancement of science and education and true learning:
Lord, let me stand to-day.

For the redemption of daily business from the blight of self-seeking:
Lord, let me stand to-day.

For the rights of the weak and the oppressed:
Lord, let me stand to-day.

For industrial co-operation and mutual help:
Lord, let me stand to-day.

For the conservation of the rich traditions of the past:
Lord, let me stand to-day.

For the recognition of new workings of thy Spirit in the minds of the men of my own time:
Lord, let me stand to-day.

For the hope of yet more glorious days to come:
Lord, let me stand to-day.

II

To-day, O Lord—

> Let me put right before interest:
> *To-day, O Lord.*

> Let me put others before self:
> *To-day, O Lord.*

> Let me put the things of the spirit before the things of the body:
> *To-day, O Lord.*

> Let me put the attainment of noble ends above the enjoyment of present pleasures:
> *To-day, O Lord.*

> Let me put principle above reputation:
> *To-day, O Lord.*

> Let me put thee before all else:
> *To-day, O Lord.*

III

To-day, O God—

> Teach me to use all the circumstances of my life that they may bring forth in me the fruits of holiness rather than the fruits of sin:
> *To-day, O God.*

> Let me use disappointment as material for patience:
> *To-day, O God.*

> Let me use success as material for thankfulness:
> *To-day, O God.*

Let me use suspense as material for perseverance:
To-day, O God.

Let me use danger as material for courage:
To-day, O God.

Let me use reproach as material for longsuffering:
To-day, O God.

Let me use praise as material for humility:
To-day, O God.

Let me use pleasures as material for temperance:
To-day, O God.

Let me use pain as material for endurance:
To-day, O God.

Morning Prayers

We give thee thanks, holy Lord, Father Almighty, eternal God, who hast been pleased to bring us through the night to the hours of morning: we pray thee graciously to grant that we may pass this day without sin, so that at eventide we may again give thanks to thee, through Jesus Christ our Lord.

Blessed be the hour, O Christ, in which thou wast born, and the hour in which thou didst die:

Blessed be the dawn of thy rising again, and the high day of thine ascending.

O most merciful and mighty Redeemer Christ, let all times be the time of our presence with thee, and of thy dwelling in us.

Grant us, O Lord, to pass this day in gladness and peace, without stumbling and without stain; that, reaching the eventide victorious over all temptation, we may praise thee, the eternal God, who art blessed, and dost govern all things, world without end.

O Lord, when I awake, and day begins, waken me to thy presence; waken me to thine indwelling; waken me to inward sight of thee, and speech with thee, and strength from thee, that all my earthly walk may waken into song and my spirit leap up to thee all day, all ways.

O Gracious Father, since it is of thy mercy that another day is added to our lives, we here dedicate both our souls and bodies to thee and thy service, in a sober, righteous, and godly life: in which resolution, do thou, O merciful God, confirm and strengthen us; that, as we grow in age, we may grow in grace, and in the knowledge of our Lord and Saviour, Jesus Christ.

O God, who hast been the refuge of my fathers through many generations, be my refuge to-day in every time and circumstance of need. Be my guide through all that is dark and doubtful. Be my guard against all that threatens my spirit's welfare. Be my strength in time of testing. Gladden my heart with thy peace; through Jesus Christ my Lord.

Into thy hands, O Lord, we commend ourselves and all who are dear to us this day. Be with us in our going out and in our coming in. Strengthen us for the work which thou hast given us to do. And grant that, filled with thy Holy Spirit, we may walk worthy of our high calling, and cheerfully accomplish those things that thou wouldest have done; through Jesus Christ our Lord.

Evening Prayers

O God, I thank thee for life and being, and for all the blessings of the past day; for the love that I have received and given, for all the kindnesses that I have received from others and for thy grace going before me and following after me. Above all I thank thee for him through whom I know of thy love and receive thy grace, even Jesus Christ, my Lord and Saviour.

O Almighty Father, who in thy divine mercy dost cover the earth with the curtain of darkness, that all the weary may rest: grant unto all men rest in thee this night. Let thy grace comfort and support all who are to spend it in sorrow, in anxiety, or in affliction. We commend into thy hands all our dear relations, friends and neighbours. Strengthen and confirm thy faithful people, convert the wicked, arouse the careless, recover the fallen, relieve the sick, give peace to the dying, guide the perplexed, and remove all hindrances to the apprehension of thy truth, that thy holy Name may be glorified in Jesus Christ, our Lord and Saviour.

Lord, ere I sleep I pray thy Spirit to cleanse and sanctify the impulses and memories of this day, that naught may go down into the depth of my being which has not been marked as thine. So give me true and holy being in the new creation of Jesus Christ, thy well-beloved Son.

O Lord God, the Life of mortals, the Light of the faithful, the strength of those who labour, and the repose of the dead, grant us a tranquil night free from all disturbance; that after an interval of quiet sleep, we may, by thy bounty, at the return of light, be endued with activity from the Holy Spirit, and enabled in security to render thanks to thee.

Into thy thands, O gracious Father, we commend ourselves, and all whom we love. Thine, O Lord, is the day, thine also is the night; cover our sins with thy mercy as thou dost cover the earth with darkness; and grant that the Sun of Righteousness may ever shine in our hearts, to chase away the darkness of all evil thoughts; through Jesus Christ our Lord.

Be present, O merciful God, and protect us through the silent hours of this night, so that we who are wearied by the changes and chances of this fleeting world, may repose upon thy eternal changelessness; through Jesus Christ our Lord.

Abide with us, O Lord, for it is toward evening and the day is far spent; abide with us, and with thy whole Church. Abide with us in the evening of the day, in the evening of life, in the evening of the world. Abide with us and with all thy faithful ones, O Lord, in time and eternity.

The World's Work

ALL IN COMMERCE AND INDUSTRY

O God, who givest to every man his work and through his labour's dost accomplish thy purpose upon earth: Grant thy blessing, we beseech thee, to those who are engaged in the industries and commerce of this land. Inspire them with the knowledge that in ministering to the needs of others they are serving thee; defend them from injustice and greed, and give them the due reward of their labours; that, seeking first thy Kingdom and righteousness, all things may be added unto them here and hereafter; through Jesus Christ our Lord.

FARMERS

Give, O Lord, to all who till the ground
    wisdom to understand thy laws,
        and to co-operate with thy wise ordering of the
           world:
and grant that the bountiful fruits of the earth
    may not be hoarded by the selfish
    or squandered by the foolish,
but that all who work may share abundantly
    in the harvest of the soil;
        through Jesus Christ our Lord.

ALL WHO ADMINISTER JUSTICE

O God, mighty and merciful, the Judge of all men: grant to those who minister justice the spirit of wisdom and discernment; and that they may be strong and patient, upright and compassionate, fill them, we beseech thee, with the spirit of thy holy fear; through Jesus Christ our Lord.

ALL WHO INFLUENCE PUBLIC OPINION

Almighty God, who hast proclaimed thine eternal truth by the voice of prophets and evangelists: Direct and bless, we beseech thee, those who in this our generation speak where many listen and write what many read; that they may do their part in making the heart of the people wise, its mind sound, and its will righteous; to the honour of Jesus Christ our Lord.

TRAVELLERS ON OUR ROADS

Almighty God, giver of life and health, guide, we pray thee, with thy wisdom all who are striving to save from injury and death the travellers on our roads. Grant to those who drive along the highways consideration for others, and to those who walk on them or play beside them thoughtful caution and care; that so without fear or disaster we all may come safely to our journey's end, by thy mercy who carest for us; through Jesus Christ our Lord.

FOR ETERNAL VALUES

Deliver us, O God, from following the fashions of the day in our thinking. Save us from the worship of power, whether power over nature or power over man; save us from the worship of science, and grant that, giving thee thanks for the skill of the scientist, we may be preserved from the abuse of his discoveries. Help us never to confuse any creature with the Creator, or man with God. May we acknowledge man's reason as thy gift and, being freed from all false hopes and misplaced trust, find in thee our hope and our salvation, through Jesus Christ our Lord.

OUR DEPENDENCE ON OTHERS

O God, who hast bound us together in this bundle of life: Give us grace to understand how our lives depend upon the courage, the industry, the honesty, and the integrity of our fellow-men; that we may be mindful of their needs, grateful for their faithfulness, and faithful in our responsibilities to them; through Jesus Christ our Lord.

ALL WHO WORK BY NIGHT

Bless, O Lord, all those who, in the night, watch over our lives and homes, and guard all who through the hours of darkness carry on the unresting commerce of men by land and sea and air. Grant them rest and refreshment, and make us thankful for their service; through Jesus Christ our Lord.

Prayers of Worship

Almighty God, whose glory the heavens are telling, the earth thy power, and the sea thy might, and whose greatness all thy creatures that think and feel everywhere proclaim: To thee belong all glory, honour, might, greatness, and splendour, now and for ever, world without end.

O my God, thou thyself art thine own praise; nor canst thou worthily be praised by any other than thyself; for of all things thou art the maker and ruler, and from thee do all things come. Ever therefore shouldst thou be praised and blessed by every creature. May every name that can be used of thee, and every word that can be spoken of thee, praise thee and magnify thee for ever.

O Almighty God, from whom every good prayer cometh, and who pourest out on all who desire it the spirit of grace and supplication: Deliver us, when we draw nigh to thee, from coldness of heart and wanderings of mind, that with steadfast thoughts and kindled affections we may worship thee in Spirit and in truth; through Jesus Christ our Lord.

My God and my Lord, thou art my hope and my heart's joy. Thou hast made me in thine image, that I may direct all my thoughts to thee, and love thee aright, that I may more and more love thee, enjoy thee, and possess thee. Let my love to thee grow in this life, and let it ripen in the life to come, my God and my Lord.

O my God, thou art good:
   There is none good but thee;
   all greatness thou art, but all goodness first.
Out of thy goodness thou madest me;
   for thy goodness I know thee;
   after thy goodness would I walk;
      to the kingdom of thy goodness, come.
My mouth shall speak of thy goodness all the day long,
   for I know no end thereof.

Blessed be thou, O God,
who hast declared that it is thine eternal purpose to
   gather in one all things in Christ.
Worthy art thou to receive honour and power and
   glory,
for the great love wherewith thou hast loved all
   mankind,
and hast delivered us from the powers of darkness,
and brought us into the kingdom of thy Son.

O God, who requirest that we should seek thee, and
makest us to find thee, and openest to us when we
knock: O God, from whom to be averted is to fall,
and to whom to be turned is to rise; in whom to abide
is to be established: O God, whom to know is to live,
whom to serve is to reign; I praise thee, I bless thee, I
adore thee, my God.

Prayers of Compassion

Watch thou, O Lord, with those who wake, or watch, or weep tonight, and give thine angels charge over those who sleep. Tend thy sick ones, O Lord Christ; rest thy weary ones; bless thy dying ones; soothe thy suffering ones; pity thine afflicted ones; shield thy joyous ones. And all, for thy love's sake.

Gracious and most merciful Father, let thy presence and peace be known wheresoever there is sickness, sorrow, or distress. Give to all tired and weary sufferers, this night, the gift of sleep; and, if sleep come not, let thy Holy Spirit bring to their remembrance thoughts of comfort from thy Word, that they may stay their minds on thee, through Jesus Christ our Lord.

O Heavenly Father, we pray thee for those suffering from diseases for which at present there is no cure. Give them the victory of trust and hope, that they may never lose their faith in thy loving purpose. Grant thy wisdom to all who are working to discover the causes of disease, and the realization that through thee all things are possible. We ask this in the Name of him who went about doing good and healing all manner of disease, even thy Son Jesus Christ our Lord.

O God our Father, we remember before thee all orphaned, homeless, and unwanted children, the children of loveless homes, and those who suffer from bodily defect and disease. Make our hearts burn within us for the children of our dark places, and teach us how to turn to good account the laws that protect them and the efforts of those who strive to succour them; through Jesus Christ our Lord.

O merciful and loving Father of all, look down, we pray thee, on the many millions who are hungry in the world to-day and are at the mercy of disease. Grant that we who have lived so comfortably and gently all our lives may have true sympathy with them and do all in our power, as individuals and as a nation, to help them to that abundant life which is thy will for them; through Jesus Christ our Lord.

O Lord Jesus Christ, who in thy last agony didst commend thy spirit into the hands of thy heavenly Father; Have mercy upon all sick and dying persons; may death be unto them the gate of everlasting life. Grant them at the last the assurance that, whether we wake or sleep, we are still with thee, through him whom thou hast given to be the resurrection and the life of all the faithful, thy Son.

O thou whose divine tenderness ever outsoars the narrow loves and charities of earth, grant me to-day a kind and gentle heart towards all things that live. Let me not ruthlessly hurt any creature of thine. Let me take thought also for the welfare of little children, and of those who are sick, and of the poor; remembering that what I do unto the least of these his brethren I do unto Jesus Christ my Lord.

Prayers for Home and Family

O Lord our God, from whom neither life nor death can separate those who trust in thy love, and whose love holds in its embrace thy children in this world and the next: so unite us to thyself that in fellowship with thee we may always be united to our loved ones whether here or there: give us courage, constancy, and hope; through him who died and was buried and rose again for us, Jesus Christ our Lord.

O God our Father, we bring before thee all those whom we love, knowing that thou dost love them more even than we do and that thy will for them is something better than we can imagine or desire. Let thy will be done in them and for them, and grant them that strength which shall make them more than conquerors, through him who loves them and us, Jesus Christ our Lord.

O God, who art everywhere present: Look down with thy mercy upon those who are absent from among us. Give thy holy angels charge over them, and grant that they may be kept safe in body, soul, and spirit, and be presented faultless before the presence of thy glory with exceeding joy; through Jesus Christ our Lord.

O God, who art present to thy faithful people in every place: Mercifully hear our prayers for those we love who are now parted from us; watch over them, we beseech thee, and protect them in anxiety, danger, and temptation; and assure both them and us that thou art always near, and that we are one in thee for ever; through Jesus Christ our Lord.

O God, the Father and defender of thy people, whom neither space nor time can separate from such as continue in thy keeping: Be present, we beseech thee, with those who are parted from us; prosper them and do them good; guide and direct them in all their undertakings; let nothing hurtful beset them and no evil befall them; and grant that, upheld by thy right hand, they may arrive in safety at their journey's end; through Jesus Christ our Lord.

Grant unto us, O God, to trust thee not for ourselves alone, but for those also whom we love and who are hid from us by the shadow of death; that, as we believe thy power to have raised our Lord Jesus Christ from the dead, so we may trust thy love to give eternal life to all who believe in him; through the same Jesus Christ our Lord.

Blessed be thou for all whom I have loved, and who have loved me: and for thy love, from all eternity, beyond compare or compass: merciful, tender, unalterable, irremovable. Blessed be thou, O Lord.

Index of Subjects